W9-DGB-459

SHAMU:

The 1st Killer Whale in Captivity

Written by Joeming Dunn • Illustrated by Brian Denham

FAMOUS FIRSTS: ANIMALS MAKING HISTORY

Making 1965 History

magic wagon

visit us at www.abdopublishing.com

Published by Magic Wagon, a division of the ABDO Publishing Group, 8000 West 78th Street, Edina, Minnesota 55439. Copyright © 2012 by Abdo Consulting Group, Inc. International copyrights reserved in all countries. All rights reserved. No part of this book may be reproduced in any form without written permission from the publisher.

Graphic Planet™ is a trademark and logo of Magic Wagon.

Printed in the United States of America, North Mankato, Minnesota.
052011
092011
This book contains at least 10% recycled materials.

Written by Joeming Dunn
Illustrated and Brian Denham
Colored by Robby Bevard
Lettered by Doug Dlin
Edited by Stephanie Hedlund and Rochelle Baltzer
Interior layout and design by Antarctic Press
Cover art by Brian Denham
Cover design by Neil Klinepier

Library of Congress Cataloging-in-Publication Data

Dunn, Joeming W.
  Shamu : the 1st killer whale in captivity / written by Joeming Dunn ; illustrated by Brian Denham.
    p. cm. -- (Famous firsts. Animals making history)
  Includes index.
  ISBN 978-1-61641-642-3
  1. Shamu (Whale)--Juvenile literature. 2. Killer whale--United States--Juvenile literature. 3. Captive marine animals--United States--History--Juvenile literature. 4. Famous animals--United States--Juvenile literature. I. Denham, Brian, ill. II. Title.
  QL737.C432D86 2012
  599.53'6--dc22
                              2011011365

TABLE OF CONTENTS

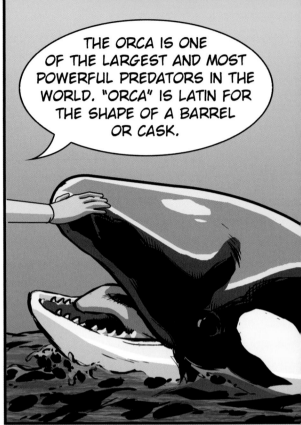

Orcas are solid black with white and gray patches. They are one the most recognized creatures in the animal kingdom. Notice the oval white patch above and behind each eye.

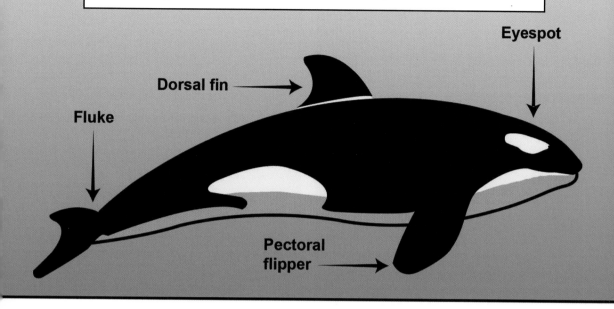

Eyespot

Dorsal fin

Fluke

Pectoral flipper

An adult male orca is very large, usually from 20 to 25 feet (6 to 8 m) long. That is about the length of a school bus. The largest killer whale ever seen was almost 32 feet (10 m) long!

Male orcas weigh 1.5 to 2 tons (1.4 to 1.8 T).

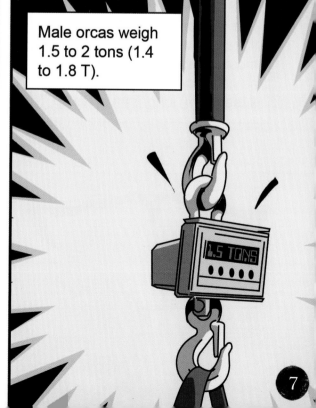

1.5 TONS

The orca's fins and flippers are specially adapted for swimming.

The pectoral flipper contains five digits, much like a human hand.

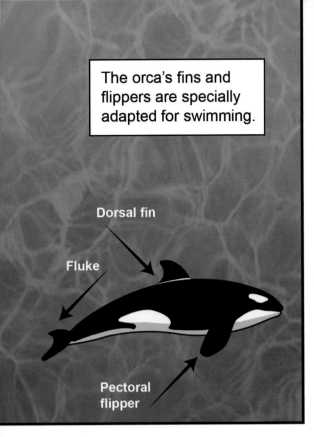

Dorsal fin

Fluke

Pectoral flipper

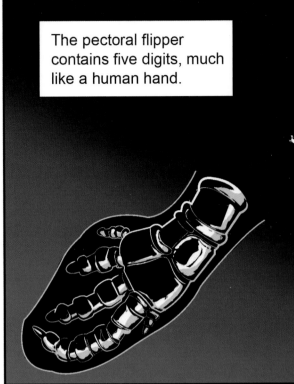

The two-lobed tail is called a fluke. An orca's fluke contains mostly tissue, but no bones. In some orcas, the fluke can reach 9 feet (3 m) long from tip to tip.

The dorsal fin helps stabilize an orca when it swims fast. In some males, this fin can reach 6 feet (2 m) tall. Like the tail, it has no bones.

All of these fins and flippers help regulate an orca's body temperature.

Despite its size, an orca can achieve great speed in the water. It can swim up to 30 miles per hour (48 km/h) for short periods of time.

That's as fast as a white-tailed deer can move on land!

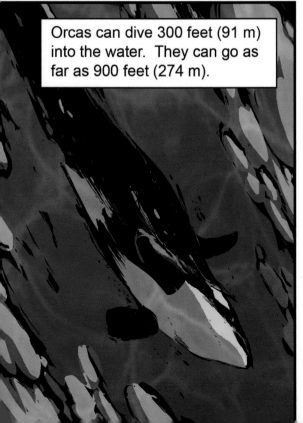

Orcas can dive 300 feet (91 m) into the water. They can go as far as 900 feet (274 m).

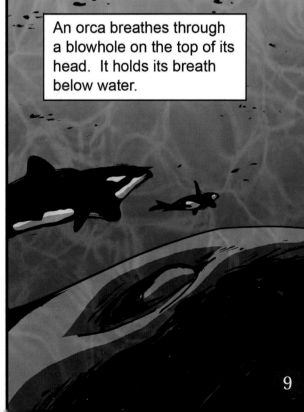

An orca breathes through a blowhole on the top of its head. It holds its breath below water.

Orcas have been found in all the oceans of the world. But, they prefer the colder waters near coasts.

The largest population of orcas lives near Antarctica. We can't be sure of the number of orcas because they live in so many places around the world.

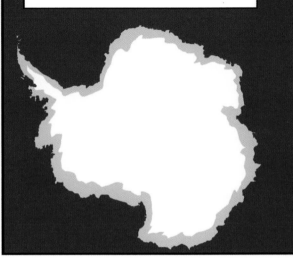

Orcas are actually part of the dolphin family. They are the largest dolphins in the world.

ONE OF THE THINGS THAT MAKE ORCAS POWERFUL PREDATORS IS THEIR TEETH.

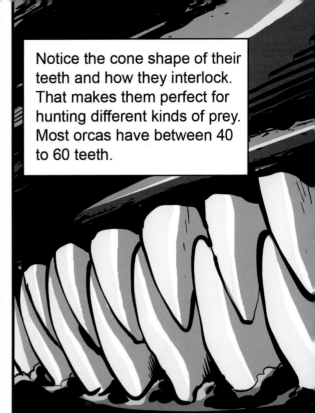

Notice the cone shape of their teeth and how they interlock. That makes them perfect for hunting different kinds of prey. Most orcas have between 40 to 60 teeth.

EACH TOOTH IS ABOUT THREE INCHES (8 CM) LONG AND ONE INCH (3 CM) THICK.

THE LIFE OF AN ORCA

MOST ORCAS BECOME ADULTS AT AROUND 15 YEARS OF AGE.

Female orcas carry babies for about 16 months. They usually give birth to a single baby, or calf. Unfortunately, most calves die within the first year of life. In some areas, only 50 percent survive.

If they survive the first year, the average life span of a female orca is 50 years. Males live about 30 years. However, many orcas live much longer than that.

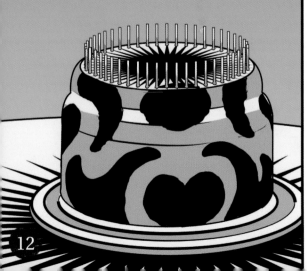

One orca was said to have lived 90 years!

MOST ORCAS LIVE IN SMALL, CLOSE-KNIT GROUPS CALLED PODS.

Pods can be different sizes. Some are as small as three orcas and some are as large as fifty!

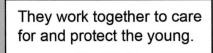

They work together to care for and protect the young.

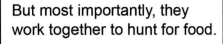

But most importantly, they work together to hunt for food.

Orcas are very good hunters.

Once the prey has been spotted, the orcas surround it.

When the prey enters the water, one orca chases it.

Then, another orca in the pod catches it.

15

For larger prey, a pod of orcas usually attacks from different angles.

Orcas can also attack individually. Sometimes they will use their tails or noses to stun their prey.

THAT IS WHAT MAKES THE ORCA ONE OF THE MOST POWERFUL PREDATORS OF THE SEA.

BEHAVIOR AND ACTIVITIES

THE ORCA HAS A WIDE VARIETY OF ACTIVITIES.

The most important of its tasks is foraging for food.

They sometimes travel great distances to look for food. There are some reports of orcas traveling up to 100 miles (161 km) in a day.

One of the most common activities performed by orcas is breaching. This is when a whale leaps high above the water.

Another is spyhopping. This is when an orca's head bobs above the water.

They also slap the water with their tails.

We're still not sure what each of these activities represents. They could be a form of communication or just simple playfulness.

Orcas have very good hearing and eyesight. They rely mostly on sound.

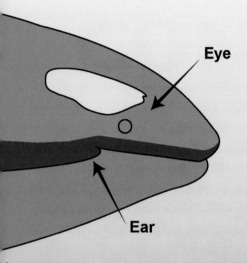

Eye

Ear

They make sound by moving air between the blowhole and nasal sacs.

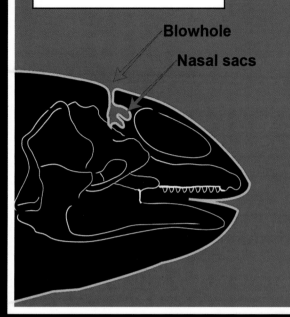

Blowhole

Nasal sacs

They use clicks, whistles, and pops to communicate, navigate, and hunt. Some say that pods form their own language with these sounds.

To help locate objects, the orca produces high-frequency sound waves and listens for the echoes.

THE HISTORY OF SHAMU

The first orca was caught in the early 1960s. Unfortunately, it passed away within a day of being captured.

Many believed it would be impossible to hold an orca in captivity.

About four years later, along the coast of Namu, Canada,...

...a male orca was tangled in some fishing nets.

The orca was named Namu, after the city near where it was found. It was sold and brought to the Seattle Aquarium.

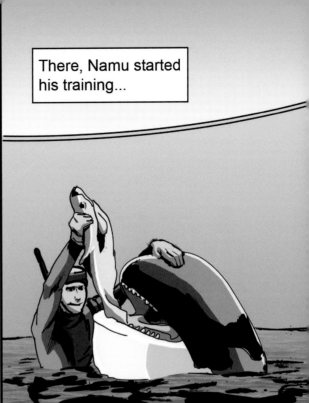

There, Namu started his training...

...and he began to learn how to perform.

In the early 1960s, four men—Milton C. Shedd, Ken Norris, David Demott, and George Millay—wanted to build an underwater restaurant.

The restaurant idea never came true. They decided to build a marine zoological park dedicated to education, research, and conservation.

On March 21, 1964, SeaWorld San Diego opened.

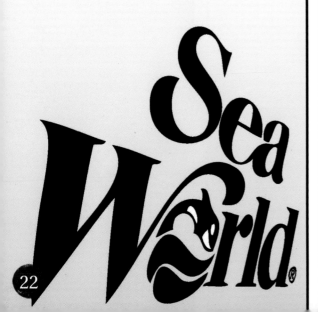

It was located in Mission Bay, San Diego. It contained sea lions, dolphins, and sea water aquariums. It was a success, drawing about 400,000 visitors in its first year.

NOW THAT YOU KNOW A BIT ABOUT ORCAS AND SEAWORLD, IT'S TIME TO LEARN ABOUT ME!

The Seattle Aquarium and SeaWorld worked together to find a female orca as a companion for Namu. And in October 1965, they were successful.

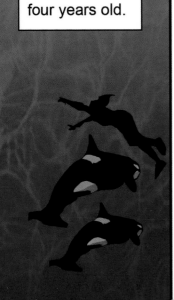

The female Orca was named Shamu, or She-Namu. She was about four years old.

Soon, they were in Seattle training with each other...

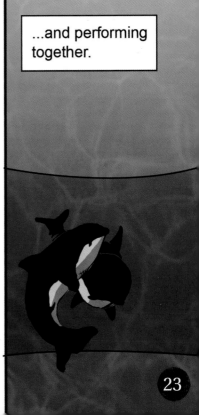

...and performing together.

23

Things did not always go very smoothly. Often, they would fight with each other.

Shamu was transported to SeaWorld San Diego in December 1965.

She performed for many years. In one performance, she attacked a SeaWorld employee named Annette Eckis. Shamu retired soon afterward.

The original Shamu passed away on August 23, 1971, after six years in captivity.

THE LEGACY OF
SHAMU

BECAUSE OF SHAMU, HUMANS HAVE LEARNED MUCH ABOUT MARINE LIFE.

On September 26, 1985, an orca was born at SeaWorld in Orlando, Florida. It was the first orca to be born and thrive in captivity.

WE DISCOVERED THEIR GREAT INTELLIGENCE, WHICH ALLOWED US TO PERFECT TRAINING TECHNIQUES.

With the success of SeaWorld, a research institute was established. An animal rescue and rehabilitation program was started, too. This allowed for the rescue of a large number of animals, including sea turtles, whales, and dolphins.

SeaWorld San Diego became the first park to breed emperor penguins outside of the Antarctic.

SeaWorld also helped develop the Oiled Wildlife Care Center. This center can care for marine life if an oil spill affects their environment.

DESPITE THE GOOD WORK OF SEAWORLD, THE CAPTIVITY OF ORCAS AND OTHER ANIMALS DOES CAUSE SOME DEBATE.

Many societies and clubs campaign against keeping animals in captivity. Their main argument is that most captive animals aren't expected to live as long.

Also, orcas can be aggressive. They have attacked other orcas and even killed some of their human trainers.

27

Today, Shamu and Namu are stage names given to orcas that live at the SeaWorld parks. They remain one of the most popular attractions at the parks, drawing over 23 million visitors a year.

SHAMU FACTS

Name: Shamu
Age at captivity: Four years old
Weight: 2,000 pounds (907 kg) at capture
Length: 14 feet (4 m) at capture
Breed: Orca

Making 1965 History

Capture date: October 1965
Capture site: Carr Inlet near Tacoma, Washington
Death: August 1971 after six years in captivity

Result: Due to Shamu's captivity, we have learned much about orcas and their behaviors, intelligence, and life cycles. Today, Shamu is the stage name for any adult female orca performing at SeaWorld parks.

WEB SITES

To learn more about Shamu, visit ABDO Group online at **www.abdopublishing.com**. Web sites about Shamu are featured on our Book Links page. These links are routinely monitored and updated to provide the most current information available.

GLOSSARY

aggressive – displaying hostility.

aquarium – a tank to hold fish or other animals.

captivity – the state of being captured and held against one's will.

conservation – the planned management of natural resources to protect them from damage or destruction. Conservation can also protect man-made resources, such as historic or cultural structures.

debate – to argue publicly about a question or a topic.

digit – a division in a limb, such as a finger or toe.

dorsal – relating to or located near or on the back, especially of an animal.

fluke – either of the two halves of a whale's tail.

forage – to search.

interlock – to connect together so that they are united.

life span – the length of time an individual exists.

lobe – a rounded projecting part, as of a body part or a leaf.

nasal sac – a space in the head of a mammal that becomes a nasal passage.

pectoral – located in or on the chest.

predator – an animal that lives by killing and eating other animals.

regulate – to fix or adjust the amount or degree of something.

rehabilitation – to restore to a condition of health or useful activity.

sound waves – a wave of vibration that carries sound.

stabilize – to keep steady.

thrive – to do well.

zoological park – a building or park that holds wild animals and exhibits them.

INDEX